Famous Firsts
of
Black Americans

Other books by Sibyl Hancock

FAMOUS FIRSTS
——OF——
Black Americans
Sibyl Hancock

Illustrations by Shelton Miles

PELICAN PUBLISHING COMPANY
GRETNA 1983

Library of Congress Cataloging in Publication Data
Hancock, Sibyl.
  Famous firsts of black Americans.

  Summary: Biographies of twenty black men
and women who made notable contributions in the
fields of science, politics, sports, and the
arts from the 1500's to the present.
  1. Afro-Americans—Biography—Juvenile
literature. 2. Afro-Americans—History—
Juvenile literature. [1. Afro-Americans—
Biography] I. Miles, Shelton, ill. II. Title.
E185.96.H23   920'.009296073 [B] [920] 82-612
ISBN 0-88289-240-1   AACR2

Manufactured in the United States of America
Published by Pelican Publishing Company
1101 Monroe Street, Gretna, Louisiana 70053

For Pauline Watson, my Louisiana friend

CONTENTS

AUTHOR'S NOTE

In doing research for a biography of Bill Pickett, published by Harcourt Brace Jovanovich, I came across so many interesting facts about black people that I decided to write about their many contributions to the culture of our world. Unfortunately these contributions often have not received the notice they deserve. This book tells about some black people who succeeded in becoming the first of their race to achieve something unusual and important in the shaping of the destiny of America.

Famous Firsts
of
Black Americans

Explorer

ESTEVANICO DORANTEZ

ESTEVANICO DORANTEZ
(Born about 1500–Died 1539)

Estevanico Dorantez was a tall black man who sailed from Spain more than four hundred years ago. He was with a group of men who were searching for new lands beyond the Atlantic Ocean. The ship was wrecked when it hit coral reefs on the Florida coast. Many crewmen died in the wreck, and unfriendly Indians killed most of the survivors. Estevanico and three Spaniards were the only ones left alive.

For eight years they traveled through swamps and deserts before finally reaching Mexico City in 1536. During this long trek, the four men lived with the Indians, and Estevanico learned to speak many Indian languages. He wore colorful clothes and often danced with the Indians, who thought of him as one of their own.

In 1539 Friar Marcos de Niza of Mexico City decided to lead an expedition to the lands to the north. He had heard stories about rich cities with streets paved with gold, the fabled Seven Cities of Cibola. He asked Estevanico to be the guide.

Estevanico traveled ahead of the main group, taking only a few Indians with him. The Indians could not speak Spanish, so Estevanico agreed to send Friar Marcos a cross made of twigs or tree branches to report his findings. A small cross would mean he had found nothing out of the ordinary. But if he found great cities he would send back a large cross.

One day two Indians brought a large cross to Friar Marcos. The Mexicans were excited. They wondered if this meant that Estevanico had found the Seven Cities of gold.

15

Friar Marcos and his men did not find the Seven Cities, but they did find a settlement of large Indian pueblos standing four stories high. Estevanico was never seen again. The Indians of the settlement had killed him because they feared he would try to conquer them. Estevanico had not found a golden city, but he had made an important discovery. He had opened the way to the territory that is now New Mexico and Arizona.

Patriot

CRISPUS ATTUCKS

18

CRISPUS ATTUCKS
(Born about 1723–Died 1770)

In 1770 the land that was to become the United States was still a group of colonies ruled by England. Bad feelings toward England developed among the colonists. For England had taxed the people heavily and had sent British troops to keep order.

Crispus Attucks did not like British rule. He had once been a slave, and he knew freedom was wonderful. Twenty years earlier he had run away from his master and become a sailor on a whaling vessel.

In the spring of 1770, Crispus came home from the sea. He decided to stay in Boston. Crispus saw that his countrymen were troubled. He began to talk with the people who gathered in the streets. He had been at sea a long time, and much had happened while he was gone.

Crispus was interested in the colonists and their resistance to England. He decided he would help them.

"Work together," he told them. "You must strike out at the British if they try to enslave you."

The crowd cheered. They agreed that they could not stand by while the British treated them unfairly.

It was on a snowy night, March 5, 1770, when Crispus Attucks led a group of men into the town square. Fire bells were ringing, but there was no fire. The bells were calling men to gather in defense of the colonists. In a disagreement with some Boston citizens, one of the British soldiers had knocked down a young boy, and tempers were short.

Crispus faced the armed soldiers. None of the colonists had guns. Suddenly someone threw a rock at the soldiers. An order was shouted—"Fire!"

Crispus Attucks was killed by the first shot. Four other men died, too, in what came to be called the Boston Massacre. The colonists would never forget the deaths of those five brave men.

Crispus Attucks was the first American black man to become famous for resisting British rule and one of the first men of any race to do so.

Scientist

BENJAMIN BANNEKER

BENJAMIN BANNEKER
(Born 1731–Died 1806)

In the days before America won her independence, many people thought blacks were not intelligent and could not learn. One of the first blacks to prove that belief wrong was Benjamin Banneker.

Benjamin was born in Maryland and raised on a farm. In those days most blacks were bought and owned by white men. They were slaves. But Benjamin was lucky because he was born a free man. His grandmother had come from England, and she taught him to read and write.

School was easy for Benjamin. He loved science and arithmetic. His teacher had to find harder problems for him to solve. When Benjamin had finished school, he wanted to go to college. But his family did not have the money to send him. Benjamin liked reading more than playing. Since there were not many books to occupy his time at home, he made up hard arithmetic problems and solved them. After a few years, people from all over the colonies heard about Benjamin, and they sent arithmetic problems for him to solve.

When Benjamin was thirty years old, a friend loaned him a pocket watch. Benjamin studied the watch and then made a clock. All of the clock's parts were made of wood, and it struck every hour. Benjamin's clock was the first striking clock ever made in America. People came from many miles away to see it, and they wanted to meet Benjamin.

Several years later, new people moved into Benjamin's neighborhood. He was happy to learn that they too liked science. One of the men loaned Benjamin a book on astronomy. The book told about the planets and stars. Benjamin studied until he became an expert in astronomy. At night he often wrapped himself in a cloak and lay in the grass, watching the stars and moon until dawn.

In 1791 President George Washington chose Benjamin to help plan the city of Washington, D.C. Benjamin was the first black to be appointed to a job by a president of the United States. The man in charge of the city's plan, Pierre L'Enfant, had an argument with federal officials and quit. He took the printed plans with him. All would have been lost, but Benjamin knew them by memory. He carefully drew the plans again for the great city.

Benjamin won even more fame when he published an almanac. His book was filled with facts about the planets, the moon, and the weather. Benjamin's forecasts were exactly right. The almanac became famous in America and in Europe.

Benjamin Banneker proved to many people the world over that blacks had the ability to make significant contributions to science and other fields of knowledge.

Pioneer

JEAN BAPTISTE POINTE DU SABLE

JEAN BAPTISTE POINTE DU SABLE
(Born about 1745–Died 1818)

Jean Baptiste Pointe du Sable was born in Haiti in 1745. His father owned a store that stocked coffee, hardwoods, and other products. Jean often worked in the store.

When Jean was grown he set sail for America. He wanted to bring his father new things to sell in his store. But the little ship never reached the distant shore. It was wrecked by a hurricane. A Danish ship rescued Jean and took him to New Orleans.

Jean was black and had never known slavery. He was horrified to see how black Americans were treated. Since he had lost all of his belongings in the wreck, Jean could not prove that he was free. He was afraid someone would say they owned him.

Jean decided he would be safer if he traveled into the wilderness. He built a small boat and traveled up the Mississippi River. He planned to trap animals and trade their furs to the Indians in return for goods.

After Jean reached St. Louis, he lived for a while with the Illinois Indians. Maybe because of his dark skin, the Indians trusted Jean more than a white man. He learned to speak their language and understand their customs. Later he went on to the Great Lakes and finally to Detroit.

Jean met a beautiful Indian girl and married her. After their son was born, Jean began looking for a better place to live. In 1772 he decided to build a trading post in an unsettled wilderness the Indians called *Chikagou*. It was near the southern end of Lake Michigan.

Business at the trading post increased quickly, and Jean brought his family to live there. He built a large house for his wife. This house was the first in the new settlement that came to be called Chicago. Jean Baptiste Pointe du Sable founded what was to become one of America's largest cities.

Poet

PHILLIS WHEATLEY

PHILLIS WHEATLEY
(Born about 1753–Died 1784)

Phillis Wheatley was born in Africa. When she was a small child she was captured by men who sold slaves. They brought her from Africa to America in a slave ship. The ship was so crowded and dirty that Phillis was sick by the time she reached America.

John Wheatley, a Boston tailor, and his wife bought Phillis. Mrs. Wheatley felt sorry for the tiny black girl. She wanted to nurse her back to health. The Wheatleys gave Phillis their last name and began to treat her as a member of their family.

Phillis learned to speak English and to read and write. She was given a room of her own. When Phillis was fourteen years old she began to write poetry. The Wheatleys were proud of her. They urged her to continue writing.

When the War for Independence broke out in the American colonies, Phillis wrote a poem about George Washington, and she sent it to him. To her joy, General Washington read it and wrote her a letter thanking her. He invited her to visit him, and Phillis did just that. She talked with him for about half an hour.

In her poem about General Washington, Phillis was the first to write that he was "first in peace." That phrase has become famous, and people often use it to describe America's first president.

When she was twenty years old, Phillis' first book of poetry was published. Many people found it hard to believe the poet was a black woman. Phillis continued her writing. She was freed before the death of Mrs. Wheatley. Five years later she married John Peters, but their life together was not happy. John Peters was a failure in business. He finally left Phillis to raise their three children by herself. Phillis had never been a strong woman, and with the burden of hard work and responsibility, she died at an early age.

Phillis Wheatley wrote beautiful poetry even in her days of sadness. She is remembered as America's first black poet.

Religious Leader

RICHARD ALLEN

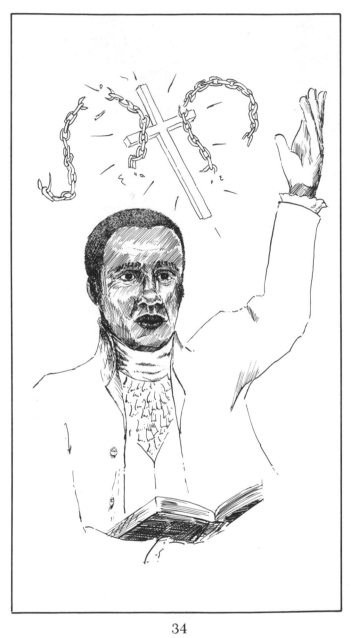

RICHARD ALLEN
(Born 1760–Died 1831)

Richard Allen was born on a plantation in Philadelphia. He was a slave, and while still a boy he was sold to a man in Delaware. As Richard grew older he became a deeply religious man. He wanted to preach and did so whenever he had the chance. His master realized that this young black man was unusually talented. He began to let Richard lead prayer services for the slaves. Later Richard preached for the family on the plantation. His master was touched by what was said, and he began to see the evils of slavery. He decided to allow his slaves to buy their freedom.

Richard worked very hard, and when he was seventeen he gained his freedom. He began to preach in churches in Delaware and other nearby states. He preached to all who came, black and white alike. Richard did not believe in separating people in church because of their race. He felt that the church was the House of God and that all men were equal in the sight of God.

Richard chose to make his home in Philadelphia, where he attended St. George's Methodist Episcopal Church. When blacks were ordered to sit apart from the whites or leave, the black Americans left the church. Richard left, too. In 1787 he formed what came to be known as the African Methodist Episcopal Church.

In 1793 a terrible epidemic of yellow fever hit Philadelphia. Many people left the city. Some of the doctors and nurses died from the disease, and there were not many people who would care for the sick. Most people were afraid of catching the disease.

35

Finally Richard Allen urged his black followers to help the city. They cared for the sick and buried the dead. It was widely believed that blacks could not catch yellow fever, but many did die from it. Later the mayor gratefully thanked the blacks for their brave services.

Richard Allen's fame as a great religious leader spread. Other ministers began to form black churches of various faiths. In 1816 Richard Allen became the first black bishop in the United States.

Explorer

YORK

YORK
(Date of birth and death unknown)

Although it is not generally known, it is a fact that a black man named York was a member of the famous Lewis and Clark Expedition of 1804–1806. York was the servant and companion of Captain William Clark.

The expedition was formed in order to learn about the lands that lay to the west beyond St. Louis. As yet Americans knew little about the great western wilderness. The men began their journey in flatboats on the Missouri River. They wanted to find out how far westward the river ran. Their orders were to study everything they saw. Lewis and Clark kept journals in which they described the Indians, animals, plants, rocks, and other interesting things they came across.

York caused much surprise among the Indians. None of them had ever seen a black man before. Some of the Indians would touch a wet finger to York's skin to see if the black would come off.

One day a fierce-looking Indian chief came to the expedition's camp. He was angry because he thought his braves had told him lies. They had said there was a black man in the expedition. York stepped forward, and the chief was amazed to see that the man *was* black. He was even more surprised when York removed his hat and let the Indian chief see his tightly curled hair. The chief finally left, ending a tense moment.

Sometimes York made friends with the Indians by dancing for them. They were also impressed by his great strength. He often made progress easier for the expedition by entertaining the Indians. York proved to be of great service during the two-year expedition. He helped tow loaded flatboats in icy waters. He was a willing and able companion.

York was the first black American to see the beauty of the Far West, including the Great Falls of the Missouri River.

Inventor

JAN MATZELIGER

JAN MATZELIGER
(Born 1852–Died 1889)

Jan Ernest Matzeliger grew up in Dutch Guiana. From an early age he had a great curiosity about machines and was always asking questions about how they operated. Jan's father put him to work in a government machine shop when he was only ten years of age.

Jan came to the United States in 1878 and settled in Massachusetts. Before long he found a job with a company that made shoes. He watched men hand-sewing the leather to the soles of the shoes. This was called *lasting*. The men were called *shoe-lasters*.

It was said that no man could ever build a machine that would last shoes. When Jan heard this, he decided to try to build just such a machine. People made fun of the young black man. They thought he was very foolish. But Jan paid no attention to them. He rented a cheap room and began experimenting at night. He used all kinds of odds and ends to build a model of his machine. He even used old cigar boxes.

Jan watched the fingers of the shoe-lasters as they stitched the leather. He worked early in the morning and late at night. He tried one idea after another. He wanted to make a machine that would do the work of the shoe-laster's fingers.

After six months of hard work, Jan finished his model machine. It was very crude, but it worked. Someone offered him fifty dollars for it, but he would not take the money. His machine did not please him enough to sell it. He thought he needed to work more on it.

Four years later Jan finished a model which could pleat the leather around the toe and heel. This time he was offered $1500, but again he refused. He wanted to build a perfect machine.

At last Jan completed his shoe-lasting machine. But all of the years of hard work and poverty had weakened Jan. His health began to fail. Not long after his marvelous machine was finished, Jan Matzeliger died.

Jan was the first man to develop a machine which could fix the leather to the sole of a shoe. This whole process took only one minute. The shoemaking industry grew enormously because of Jan's invention. He built a machine that people had said could never be built.

Bulldogger

BILL PICKETT

BILL PICKETT
(Born about 1860–Died 1932)

Bill Pickett spent the early years of his life in southern Texas. He enjoyed the rugged life of the western cowboy. Bill rode horses and roped cattle. He learned how to handle a horse with great skill.

When Bill was almost forty years old, he moved to Oklahoma and began working for the famous 101 Ranch. The cowhands of the 101 were experts in their trade. They won prizes almost every time they competed in cowboy contests.

Bill Pickett knew how to bulldog a steer. He would jump off his horse and grab the steer's horns. He twisted the steer's head around until he forced the steer to fall over. People said that Bill was the best bulldogger they had ever seen. The tall black cowboy excited crowds with his courage and strength.

The owner of the 101 Ranch decided to put on a big rodeo. His cowhands were special, and he wanted to show them off. Will Rogers was one of the cowhands, and he did wonderful rope tricks. Another was Tom Mix, who was a fine horseman and later became a movie star.

But the biggest attraction of all was Bill Pickett. He was not afraid of the wild steers. After he had thrown a bull to the ground, he would often stare right into its face. The bull was usually too afraid of Bill to charge at him.

The 101 cowhands took their show to the famous Madison Square Garden in New York City. On opening night when the time came for Bill Pickett to try to catch his steer, the animal raced ahead of his horse. The steer crossed the arena and jumped a gate. It raced up the steps into the crowd. Bill

47

followed close behind and grabbed the steer's horns. Will Rogers managed to rope the animal. With Bill hanging onto the steer's horns, Will Rogers pulled the steer back into the arena. The crowd had never seen such excitement.

Bill performed his bulldogging act all over the world. He toured Mexico, Canada, and Europe with the 101 Ranch rodeo show. Everyone wanted to see the famous black cowboy.

Bill Pickett died when he was seventy years old. He has been honored in the Cowboy Hall of Fame as the first bulldogger.

Scientist

GEORGE WASHINGTON
CARVER

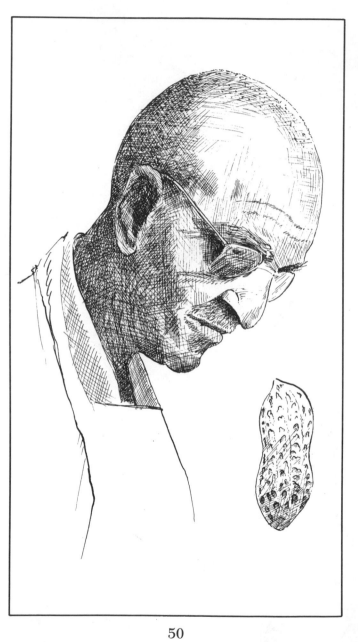

GEORGE WASHINGTON CARVER
(Born 1860–Died 1943)

George Washington Carver was born a slave in Missouri in 1860. He never knew his father or mother. When he was very young his mother was kidnapped by slave raiders. His father had been accidentally killed on a nearby farm before his mother disappeared.

Although the Civil War ended slavery, George remained on the plantation where his parents had worked. His master realized George was bright, and he sent him to a town where George could go to school. George worked on a farm to support himself. When he finished high school, he decided to go to college. His grades were always excellent.

Many colleges turned George away, but Simpson College in Iowa took him as their first black student. He later went to another college and studied agriculture. After he graduated, he became a college teacher.

George was worried about the poor people of the South. He believed that their future was in farming and learning to make new products from natural resources. After conducting many experiments, George developed more than three hundred products from the peanut. He learned to make plastics, soap, ink, and even milk—all by using the simple, common peanut plant.

George also developed products from sweet potatoes and wood shavings. Sometimes he made products by using cotton stalks. No one had ever thought the peanut was worth anything. People had said only monkeys ate peanuts, but the farmers listened to George. They planted peanuts and sweet potatoes, and before long these became two of the most important crops in the South.

Businesses offered George money to use his inventions, but George was not interested in becoming rich. He could have had a great fortune. He won many honors in the course of his life. Before he died, George used all of his savings to establish a foundation for scientific research.

People all over the world loved and respected George Washington Carver. He was the first man to discover so many useful products from something as common as the peanut.

Explorer

MATTHEW HENSON

MATTHEW HENSON
(Born 1866–Died 1955)

Matthew Henson was born on a farm in Maryland in 1866. He was two years old when his mother died. After a while his father married again, and Matthew soon found that his stepmother was going to make his life unpleasant. Matthew was eight when his father died. After his father's death, Matthew's stepmother kept him from going to school. She made him work hard and sometimes gave him whippings.

When he was eleven, Matthew ran away from home. He managed to travel all the way to the city of Washington by himself. He worked there for two years, but he soon decided he wanted to see more of the world.

Matthew was thirteen years old when he found a job on a boat docked at Baltimore. He became the captain's cabin boy. The captain was a kind man who taught Matthew to read and write as the ship sailed to distant ports. He gave Matthew many books to read.

Matthew learned much about people all over the world. He understood their customs and some of their languages. He enjoyed sailing but left the ship after his beloved captain died. After trying to work on other ships, Matthew finally gave up being a seaman. With his kind captain no longer near to protect him, Matthew had learned how badly a black man was often treated.

Several years later when Matthew was twenty-one, he took a job in a men's clothing store. It was here that Robert Peary, a naval engineer, met him. Peary hired Matthew as his personal servant to go with him to Central America. Matthew did not want to be a servant, but he wanted more than anything to travel. He took the job.

Later Peary decided to try to go all the way to the North Pole. No man had ever been there. Matthew went with him, but not as a servant. Peary hired him as a member of the expedition.

In 1888 the men set out on their first attempt to reach the North Pole, but they failed. For years they tried to reach the Pole and failed again and again. Matthew went along each time. Cold winds and storms held them back. Sometimes people were hurt. Peary broke his leg once, and another time Matthew fell into icy water and nearly froze.

Finally in 1909 Peary chose Matthew and four Eskimos to make what became the final dash to the Pole. Matthew had proven to be indispensable on these expeditions. He could speak to the Eskimos easily, and he could drive the dog teams well. He had withstood the terrible hardships of the severe cold without complaining.

When the North Pole was at last in sight, Peary handed Matthew the American flag and told him to plant it in the frozen ground. Matthew became the first man to set foot upon the North Pole.

Scientist

CHARLES HENRY TURNER

CHARLES HENRY TURNER
(Born 1867–Died 1923)

As a boy, Charles H. Turner was always interested in nature. He often lay on the ground watching ants as they moved about their anthills. The ants sometimes traveled far from their hills but never got lost. Charles wanted to know why. And he wondered why animals behaved as they did.

Charles was born in Cincinnati, Ohio, in 1867. His father was a church custodian and his mother was a nurse. Charles' father, who loved to read, collected hundreds of books. Young Charles shared his father's hunger for knowledge, and he was fortunate to have so many books from which to learn.

Charles finished his college studies at the University of Cincinnati. He began to devote his time to scientific research, as well as teaching young black people. In 1907 he was awarded a Doctor of Philosophy degree by the University of Chicago in recognition of his discoveries in the field of animal behavior.

In 1908 Dr. Charles Turner moved his family to St. Louis, where he began teaching biology at Sumner High School. His children grew up surrounded by roaches, snakes, ants, bees, and many other creatures in their father's laboratories.

Some of Dr. Turner's most important work was on the behavior of insects. He discovered that ants use light rays to guide them in finding their way back home. When he removed the light from one side of a container of ants, they began to panic and acted as if they were lost. But as soon as he turned the light on the far side of the container, the ants moved toward that side—the one that was not dark.

Dr. Turner made many original discoveries about the behavior of insects. He found that burrowing bees memorize the area around their home so that they will not get lost returning. He discovered that honeybees can tell one color from another and one pattern from another. He learned that ant lions play dead when startled, and that cockroaches can learn, especially young ones. Dr. Turner also proved that insects can hear.

Scientists and nature lovers owe much to the work of this always humble man who never had expensive laboratories. He made his discoveries with only a small salary and a brilliant mind.

Musician

W. C. HANDY

W. C. HANDY
(Born 1873–Died 1958)

William Christopher Handy was born in Florence, Alabama, in 1873. He grew up in the warm southland listening to bullfrogs croaking along the bayous and crickets chirping in the night. William enjoyed the birds singing and the lowing of the cattle in the evening as they came home from the pasture.

In school William soon found that his favorite subject was music. Before long he was trying to make up music of his own. He played tunes on a fine-tooth comb. But William's father was a Methodist minister and believed that musical instruments were instruments of the devil. He would not allow even a piano in his church.

When William was twelve, he worked as a water boy in a rock quarry. He saved his money to buy a guitar he had seen in a store. When he finally bought it and took it home, his father made him return it. William had to buy a dictionary instead.

William listened to visiting musicians play. He went to circuses and heard the exciting melodies. He wanted more than anything to become a musician.

When William finished his schooling, he went to work at a foundry in Bessemer. While he was there, he organized a band, and he played a trumpet on Sundays in the church choir. William lost his job when a depression came, and in 1896 he joined Mahara's Colored Minstrels, a traveling minstrel show. He was at last a professional musician.

William's talent as a musician developed quickly. He trained other musicians, wrote arrangements

63

for new tunes, and played solos in shows. His minstrel training paid off when he moved to Memphis in 1903 to take charge of a band. W. C. Handy, as he was now called, was convinced that people would enjoy hearing black American music.

Handy wrote a campaign song for a man running for mayor. His song, "Mr. Crump," reflected his memories of the rhythms of the uneducated black people. The song was a hit, and, after the campaign was over, the title was changed to "The Memphis Blues." Published in 1912, this was the first famous American blues song.

The next song Handy wrote was to be his most famous—"The Saint Louis Blues." The song came from his memories of river songs he had heard on the levee, of lonely nights away from home, and of people he had known. "The Saint Louis Blues" has been recorded over four hundred different times and all over the world.

W. C. Handy wrote many other songs and went on to become one of the most famous musicians of all time. He will always be remembered as the "Father of the Blues."

Boxer

JACK JOHNSON

JACK JOHNSON
(Born 1878–Died 1946)

Jack Johnson was born in Galveston, Texas, in 1878. He learned to defend himself at an early age. Most black boys had to be strong and able to fight. It was not easy to grow up being poor and black.

Jack decided he wanted to be a boxer. He practiced hour after hour building his strength. He wanted to be the best boxer in the world. In 1897 Jack began his career by knocking out his first opponent. After that he fought many more fights. Each time Jack went into the boxing ring he learned a little more.

In 1908 Jack defeated Tommy Burns in Australia. Jack Johnson became the first black heavyweight champion of the world. Jack had barely won the world title when many white people began searching for someone to defeat him. It just did not seem right to some that a black man should be the champion. Every time a new challenger was found, people called him the "white hope." Many people hoped the new fighter would beat Jack and thus take the championship away from the black man.

After holding the championship for seven years, Jack was defeated in Cuba in 1915. Although he no longer held the title of champion, Jack kept boxing. He was sixty-seven when he fought his last fight. In his long career, Jack fought in 113 fights. There are experts who say Jack Johnson was the greatest heavyweight of all time. He was elected to boxing's Hall of Fame in 1954.

Merchant Marine Captain

HUGH MULZAC

HUGH MULZAC
(Born 1886–Died 1971)

Hugh Nathaniel Mulzac was born in the British West Indies in 1886. He lived on the island of St. Vincent and always enjoyed watching the ships at sea. He decided he wanted to be a sailor. After he finished high school, Hugh attended a nautical school in South Wales. He studied ocean navigation—how to sail the seas.

When Hugh was a teen-ager he signed on with a Norwegian sailing vessel. This was his first voyage, and the first port at which he came ashore was a town in North Carolina. Hugh decided to go to church on Sunday morning, and his captain went with him. Hugh was eager to meet Americans. But when he arrived at the church, he was turned away because he was black. Hugh's captain refused to go into the church without the young black man. He said that he would not attend a church where all were not welcome. This was the first time Hugh had been treated badly because of his race.

Hugh traveled around the world. He read all the good books he could find about the countries he visited. By the time Hugh was twenty-five he had learned enough to become a second mate. He had also become a United States citizen.

Hugh served in World War I carrying war supplies across the ocean. After the war he had a hard time finding work, even though by then he was qualified to become a captain. Once he had to take a job painting houses. When World War II began, the federal government made it easier for blacks to enter service in the merchant marine. In 1942 Captain Hugh Mulzac took command of the

Booker T. Washington. The ship's crewmen were both black and white, and this pleased Captain Mulzac. He believed people should work together without thought of race.

The *Booker T. Washington* was a merchant marine ship. During World War II Captain Mulzac became famous for dodging submarines. He transported eighteen thousand soldiers and prisoners and thousands of tons of equipment across the Atlantic Ocean without losing a single man. Captain Mulzac was the first black man to be the captain of a merchant marine ship.

Inventor

FREDERICK McKINLEY JONES

FREDERICK McKINLEY JONES
(Born 1892–Died 1961)

Frederick McKinley Jones was born in Cincinnati in 1892. He was orphaned when he was nine years old, and he had to quit school after finishing the sixth grade. He found a job and worked hard to support himself.

Frederick was always interested in taking machines apart and putting them together again. As he grew older he enjoyed designing racing cars that he drove on racetracks. Frederick's name drew attention in the 1920s when he invented some machine parts that made it possible for silent movie projectors to run films with sound. His invention was much better and cheaper than one already on the market.

In 1935 Frederick began work on the invention that was to make him famous. One day his employer was playing golf with a farmer. The farmer complained that he had lost many truckloads of his crops because they had spoiled during the shipping. Frederick's employer said that perhaps his company could build a truck to solve the problem of food's spoiling while it was being taken across the country. When Frederick heard what his employer had told the farmer, he began putting old odds and ends of machinery together. When he had finished building his machine, he attached it to a truck.

Frederick had created the first mechanically refrigerated truck. This meant that food could be shipped longer distances across the country without spoiling. Fresher and better food would be awaiting the American people in stores. Frederick's invention was a success. His employer formed a company to make the new machines. Frederick became the vice-president of the company.

Frederick's mechanical refrigerating system was soon placed in ships and railway cars. And today that same system is used to transport rocket fuel. The American people would not enjoy many of the good foods they eat if it were not for Frederick Jones' wonderful invention.

Medical Researcher

CHARLES RICHARD DREW

CHARLES RICHARD DREW
(Born 1904–Died 1950)

Charles Richard Drew was born in Washington, D.C., in 1904. He lived in a section of the city where the streets were not paved and the houses needed repairing. Charles wanted to be someone important someday. But his friends laughed. He was black, they said, and blacks could never get good jobs.

Charles decided to go to college. He studied hard in high school. When he graduated, his grades were the best in his class. Amherst College accepted Charles. He became a star athlete in both football and track.

Before Charles finished college, he learned that it really did not matter whether or not he was a star athlete. People still did not want to eat with him or sit in a movie beside him because he was black. Charles wanted to become a medical doctor, so he went to a school in Canada where people did not dislike blacks. He made better grades than he had ever made at Amherst.

While he was studying to be a doctor, Charles began working on experiments with blood. Blood is made up of red cells, white cells, and plasma. He knew that if you let a bottle of blood stand for a while, it separates into two parts. The red cells and white cells sink to the bottom of the bottle. The top part of the bottle is filled with a clear liquid, which is called plasma. Plasma carries the cells to all parts of a person's body.

After Charles received his degree as a Doctor of Medicine, he kept working with blood plasma. Doctors knew that sometimes when plasma was fed into a person's veins, it saved his life. Often

79

people who are badly burned need plasma.

Dr. Drew continued experimenting until he discovered how to keep plasma from spoiling. He found that plasma could be dried. Later the dried plasma could be mixed with water, and it would be as good as new. In 1940 Dr. Drew presented his findings based on two years of research. He had made a significant discovery—how to preserve plasma.

Dr. Drew and his fellow workers began to solve problems in storing blood. They added chemicals to it and tried using different shapes of bottles. Finally Dr. Drew helped organize a blood bank where thousands of bottles of blood and plasma could be stored. Many lives have been saved due to this great man's discoveries and hard work.

Statesman

RALPH BUNCHE

RALPH BUNCHE
(Born 1904–Died 1971)

Ralph Johnson Bunche was born in Detroit, Michigan, in 1904. His father was a barber who tried very hard to earn a living for his family, but they were quite poor. When Ralph was eight years old, he sold newspapers to help add to his family's income. Both his mother and his father were in bad health. The family moved to New Mexico, hoping that the climate would help Ralph's parents. But nothing seemed to do any good, and both Ralph's mother and father died when he was eleven. Ralph went to live with his grandmother. She was a small woman and very wise. She always told him that his color had nothing to do with his worth.

When he graduated from high school, Ralph thought he should find a job and earn money to support his grandmother, but she told him to go to college. He won a scholarship to college, and by working as a janitor, he managed to save a little money. Ralph won very high honors in college, and his neighbors collected money to help him while he went to graduate school at Harvard. Ralph earned a Doctor of Philosophy degree in political science and began working for the government. He was appointed to some very important jobs, and he became well known in the United States.

When World War II began, Ralph helped the United States plan military bases in Africa. He understood the people of Africa and their customs. His advice was quite important. In 1949 the United Nations asked Ralph to try to help bring peace between the Arabs and the Jews. After many days of difficult negotiations, the countries agreed to a temporary peace. Both the Arabs and the Jews praised Dr. Bunche for his work on the settlement.

In 1950 Dr. Ralph Bunche was awarded the Nobel Peace Prize. He was the first black person to receive this high award. Later, Dr. Bunche was appointed an undersecretary of the United Nations. This is one of the most important jobs in the United Nations. Dr. Bunche always worked for peace among all races of the world.

Opera Singer

MARIAN ANDERSON

MARIAN ANDERSON
(Born 1908– 1993)

Marian Anderson was born in Philadelphia in 1908. She has said that she always loved music. When she was still very small she began to show an interest in singing. Her father was an usher in the church their family attended every Sunday. Marian was eight years old when she began singing in the church choir.

When she was twenty-two, Marian was awarded a fellowship which paid for a year of study in Europe. She sang in Paris, and the people there thought she had a wonderful voice.

Marian came back to the United States and gave concerts, but she never made much money. She decided to return to Europe, where she gave a great many concerts. She even sang before kings and queens. In each of the countries in which she sang, the audiences loved her. When the famous orchestra conductor, Arturo Toscanini, heard Marian sing, he said that a voice such as hers appeared only once in a century. A composer in Finland thought her voice so beautiful that he dedicated a composition to her.

When Marian came home to America in 1935, she was at last given the attention she deserved. She was a success everywhere she sang. Her voice had a lovely quality of richness, and she could sing both high notes and low notes easily.

Marian received many honors. However, in 1939 something unfortunate happened. A women's organization refused to let her sing in Constitution Hall in Washington, D.C., because she was black. So Marian sang instead on the steps of the Lincoln

Memorial. It was an Easter morning, and seventy-five thousand people came to see and hear her. They wanted her to know they did not approve of the cruel treatment she had received. Millions of people listened to her on the radio. She gave a great performance.

In 1955 Marian sang with the Metropolitan Opera Company. She was the first black person selected to sing regularly for the famous company. When Marian had been a little girl, she had never dreamed she would sing opera. She could not have imagined what beautiful costumes she would wear on the stage, or how many thousands of people would come to see her perform.

In 1963 Marian received the Presidential Medal of Freedom. Two years later she was elected to the Woman's Hall of Fame. Marian announced in 1965 that she was going to retire from giving concerts. When she finished her last concert at Carnegie Hall, the audience applauded with such enthusiasm that she sang an extra hour. Even then, when she left the stage she was applauded for another thirty minutes. Marian Anderson is regarded as one of the greatest singers of all time.

Baseball Player

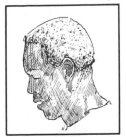

JACKIE ROBINSON

JACKIE ROBINSON
(Born 1919–Died 1972)

Jack Roosevelt Robinson was born in Georgia. He was the youngest child in his family, and he had three brothers and one sister. When Jackie was a baby, his father died. Jackie's mother moved her family to California to live with her brother. He grew very fond of the children, and after a time they came to think of him as a father.

Sports was always a favorite interest with Jackie. His oldest brother was an athlete who could run fast and excelled at the broad jump. Jackie hoped he would someday be as talented as his brother in sports.

Jackie entered high school when he was four-teen. It was not long before he became a star athlete. He liked sports of all kinds. He was on the basketball, football, baseball, and track teams.

When Jackie went to college, he set a new junior college record for the broad jump. Jackie had planned to continue going to school so that he could become a physical education teacher. But in his last year of college, Jackie had to quit. His uncle was ill and could not work. Jackie's mother had to stay home to take care of her brother. There was no more money for college.

When World War II began, Jackie joined the army. Before long an old football injury began to bother him, and after two years he was discharged from the army. Jackie began to play baseball for the Kansas City Monarchs, a team in the Black American League. He was an excellent player.

Baseball scouts watched Jackie. They liked the way he played. Some of them asked him to take a

91

trip to New York to talk about joining the Brooklyn Dodgers. Jackie decided to join the New York team.

The first year Jackie played in the major leagues was not an easy one for him. Many people felt that a black man had no place in major league baseball. Jackie paid no attention to those who were unfriendly. He played baseball the best he could and helped his team win the pennant. In 1947 Jackie was named Rookie of the Year. And in 1949 he was named the Most Valuable Player in the National League. He was made a member of the Baseball Hall of Fame in 1962.

Jackie Robinson was the first black man to play in the major leagues. He helped make playing major league baseball possible for many others of his race.

Further Suggested Reading

Bontemps, Arna Wendell. *Famous Negro Athletes.* Dodd, Mead & Co., 1964.

Bruner, Richard. *Black Politicians.* David McKay Co., Inc., 1971.

Garrett, Romero B. *Famous First Facts About Negroes.* Arno Publishing Co., 1972.

Hayden, Robert C. *Eight Black American Inventors.* Addison-Wesley Publishing Co., Inc., 1972.

_____. *Seven Black American Scientists.* Addison-Wesley Publishing Co., 1970.

Hughes, Langston. *Famous American Negroes.* Dodd, Mead & Co., 1954.

_____. *Famous Negro Heroes of America.* Dodd, Mead & Co., 1958.

_____. *Famous Negro Music Makers.* Dodd, Mead & Co., 1955.

Katz, William Loren. *Black People Who Made The Old West.* Crowell Junior Books, 1977.

_____. *The American Negro—His History And Literature.* Arno Publishing Co., 1968.

Richardson, Ben Albert. *Great Black Americans.* Crowell Junior Books, 1976.

Rollins, Charlemae Hill. *Famous American Negro Poets.* Dodd, Mead & Co., 1965.

_____. *They Showed The Way.* Crowell Junior Books, 1964.

Shepherd, Elizabeth. *The Discoveries Of Esteban The Black.* Dodd, Mead & Co., 1970.

Simmons, William J. *Men Of Mark: Eminent, Progressive And Rising.* Arno Publishing Co., 1968.

Stratton, Madeline Robinson. *Negroes Who Helped Build America.* Ginn & Co., 1965.

Stull, Edith. *Unsung Black Americans.* Grossett & Dunlap, Inc., 1971.